P9-DBT-567

WITHDRAWN

Unicorns and other Magical Creatures

by John Hamilton

Published by ABDO Publishing Company, 4940 Viking Drive, Suite 622, Edina, Minnesota 55435.
Copyright ©2005 by Abdo Consulting Group, Inc. International copyrights reserved in all countries.
No part of this book may be reproduced in any form without written permission from the publisher.
ABDO & Daughters™ is a trademark and logo of ABDO Publishing Company.

Printed in the United States.

Editor: Paul Joseph
Graphic Design: John Hamilton
Cover Design: TDI
Cover Illustration: *White Unicorn* ©1993 Don Maitz
Interior Photos and Illustrations: p 1 *The Lady With the Unicorn*, Corbis; p 4 *The Maiden and the Unicorn*, Corbis; p 5 *White Unicorn* ©1993 Don Maitz; p 6 unicorns and lions relief sculpture, Corbis; p 7 *Unicorn & Moon* ©1980 Janny Wurts; p 8 (top) detail from *Historia naturalis*, Corbis; p 8 (bottom) rhinoceros, Corbis; p 9 unicorn drinking from river, Corbis; p 10 lion fighting unicorn relief sculpture, Corbis; p 11 *Tryptich Unicorn* ©1980 Janny Wurts; p 12 coat of arms, Corbis; pp 12-13 *Unicorn in Forest* ©1976 Janny Wurts; p 14 unicorn captured, Corbis; p 15 *The Unicorn in Captivity*, Corbis; p 16 unicorn hunt, Corbis; p 17 unicorn statue at Casa Loma, Corbis; p 18 (top right) *The Last Unicorn* book cover, courtesy Roc Publishing; p 18 (bottom left) *Harry Potter and the Sorcerer's Stone* cover, courtesy Listening Library; p 19 unicorn crossing stream, Corbis; p 20 narwhal, courtesy narwhal.info; p 21 *Unicorn Walking Towards Waterfall*, Corbis; p 22 (upper right) Pegasus, Corbis; p 22 (lower left) *Starflight*, ©1979 Janny Wurts; p 23 (top right) *Gryphon*, ©1979 Janny Wurts; p 23 (bottom left) *Fireflight* ©1980 Janny Wurts; p 24 *Jeff's Gryphon* ©2004 Don Maitz; p 25 *To Ride Hell's Chasm* ©2003 Janny Wurts; p 26 *Mariner's Delerium* ©1979 Janny Wurts; p 27 mermaid, man in canoe, Corbis; pp 28-29 *Chasing the Wind* ©1996 Don Maitz; p 30 coat of arms, Corbis; p 31 *To Ride Hell's Chasm*, book cover spine ©2003 Janny Wurts.

Library of Congress Cataloging-in-Publication Data

Hamilton, John, 1959–
    Unicorns & other magical creatures / John Hamilton.
        p. cm. — (Fantasy & folklore)
    ISBN 1-59197-715-0
    1. Unicorns. 2. Animals, Mythical. I. Title: Unicorns and other magical creatures. II. Title.

GR830.U6 H36 2004
398'.469—dc22

                                                                    2004043689

CONTENTS

UNICORNS

People love unicorns. They are wonderful, mysterious creatures of fantasy. For centuries stories have been told of these noble animals. Unicorns represent many things that people value. They are fast as lightning and sure on their feet. They are intelligent, strong, and powerful, yet at the same time gentle and pure. But if provoked, these splendid animals become fierce fighters. It is almost impossible to capture a unicorn by force.

What exactly is a unicorn? Through the ages, they have come in several shapes and sizes. Today, the most common description of a unicorn is of a large, white horse with a single spiraling horn on its forehead, ending in a sharp point. In early stories of unicorns, however, the beast was described in many ways: a white body with a purple head; the tail of a lion; the hind legs of an antelope; the beard of a goat.

There is no evidence that unicorns actually lived. But that hasn't stopped people from believing in them. During the Middle Ages especially, people were convinced that these magnificent beasts were as real as the sun and moon. Even today, some people think unicorns still live in far-away lands, hidden from the prying eyes of the modern world.

Far right: Fantasy illustrator Don Maitz's *White Unicorn.*
Below: The Maiden and the Unicorn, by Domenichino.

Unicorn Origins

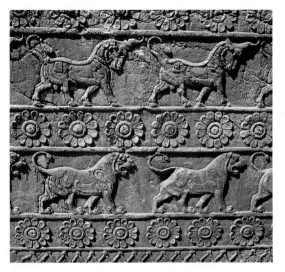

Unicorn legends go back thousands of years. They appear in ancient artwork from Mesopotamia and India. In China, unicorns are called ki-lin. They are symbols of good fortune. To the Chinese, unicorns are supernatural beings that live in the heavens, along with three other "immortals:" the dragon, the phoenix, and the turtle. Together, these creatures rule the heavens as well as parts of the earth. Unicorns rule the land animals. The Chinese unicorn is gentle and kind, and refuses to use his horn as a weapon. When a unicorn appears, the Chinese believe, it signals the birth of a great or wise person. Pictures of unicorns are sometimes posted in people's houses when a baby is expected, in the hope that the unicorn will bring good luck.

In ancient Greek literature, unicorns were described by the historian Ctesia around 400 B.C. Ctesia got his information while living in Persia. The Persians told him of a large, single-horned beast that came from India.

Left: Unicorns and lions on a relief-sculpture found at the ancient Persian capital of Persepolis, in Iran.
Far right: Unicorn & Moon by Janny Wurts.

LVXVRIA.

Ctesia wasn't the only Western scholar to hear of unicorns. Pliny the Elder was a Roman naturalist who wrote an encyclopedia of natural history more than 300 years before Ctesia. He had also heard of strange, single-horned horse-like creatures roaming the unexplored reaches of exotic India. In *Historia naturalis*, Pliny wrote, "The Indians hunt an exceedingly wild beast called the monoceros, which has a stag's head, elephant's feet, and a boar's tail, the rest of its body being like that of a horse. It makes a deep lowing noise, and one black horn two cubits (3 feet, or .9 m) long projects from the middle of its forehead. This animal, they say, cannot be taken alive."

Other Greek and Roman writers, including Aristotle and Aelian, also wrote about unicorns. Even Marco Polo, the

Above: A page from Pliny's *Historia naturalis,* the ancient text in which a unicorn-like beast is described.

Right: Was the rhinoceros mistaken for a unicorn in ancient times?

thirteenth-century Italian explorer, wrote about unicorns during his travels in the Orient. To these scholars and explorers, the existence of unicorns was an established fact, even though few of them ever claimed to have actually *seen* a unicorn.

Some people today believe these ancient scholars were actually writing about the Indian rhinoceros. Another possible real-life source of the unicorn myth is the narwhal, the "unicorn of the sea."

Another theory for unicorn myths also explains why unicorns were sighted so often in India and other Asian countries. To Western scholars, the Far East was exotic and strange, just like the unicorn. Many unicorn myths had already been established in Asia, especially China. After Western explorers and traders made contact with peoples of the East, they brought back the unicorn stories and myths. After many years of telling and retelling the stories, fiction became fact. In the days before mass media, or even the scientific method, where proof is needed before something is labeled "fact," unicorns were known by people to be real animals.

Below: A unicorn drinks from a river in this illustration by Buddy Mays.

The Symbol of the Unicorn

In ancient Mesopotamian legend, the unicorn was a symbol for the moon as it waged a never-ending battle with the sun for control of the sky. The sun was symbolized by a lion. The lion always wins the battle, but his victory is never complete. The very next night, the unicorn returns for another challenge. This ancient story may explain why unicorns are often shown together with lions.

In the Middle Ages, books often told stories of unicorns doing battle with lions. In one often-told tale, a unicorn fiercely charges at a lion. The lion steps aside, and the unicorn rams his horn in a tree, where it remains stuck. The lion then eats the unicorn. This little story is meant to show that even if you are fierce and brave, you can be beaten by your own foolishness unless you are careful.

Right: An ancient Persian relief sculpture showing a lion battling a unicorn.
Far right: Tryptich Unicorn by Janny Wurts.

Above: The Royal Coat of Arms of the United Kingdom of Great Britain and Northern Ireland.

During the Middle Ages, the people of Scotland and England identified with the fiercely loyal unicorn. Legend says that a unicorn will fight to the death rather than be captured. To the Scottish especially, this symbolized a fierce devotion and loyalty to their country. When England and Scotland were later joined under one rule in the seventeenth century, a unicorn and a lion appeared on the royal coat of arms of Great Britain.

Unicorns are also important symbols of purity and goodness in religious texts, especially Christianity. Some other faiths have also used the unicorn as a symbol, including the Zoroastrian religion, which is from ancient Persia (modern-day Iran). Buddhists use the horn of a unicorn to symbolize the highest spiritual state, known as Nirvana. To Buddhists, the unicorn shows perfection and contentment, a peaceful state that all Buddhists try to attain.

Early Christians viewed the unicorn as a symbol of Jesus Christ because both are spiritually pure and gentle. A collection of animal stories called the *Physiologus* was written about 200 A.D. It told of many similarities between unicorns and Jesus. Over the centuries the stories were translated and circulated widely in medieval Europe, where they were very popular. People loved unicorns, just as they loved Jesus, because they helped others, and because they died to purify people of their sins.

Because of this religious connection, unicorns appeared in a great deal of medieval and Renaissance works of art, including many in which unicorns appear with the Virgin Mary. Starting in the mid-sixteenth century, however, leaders in the Catholic Church decided that it was improper to show unicorns in religious artwork. Without church support, artwork of unicorns gradually fell. Today unicorns are seen mostly in secular, or popular, art, without the religious symbolism.

Right: Unicorn in Forest, by Janny Wurts.

HUNTING FOR UNICORN HORN

During the Middle Ages in Europe, unicorn stories became very popular. They were spread by religion and folklore. Unicorns appeared on many medieval paintings and tapestries. People began adding to the unicorn's legend. The unicorn's horn, in addition to its usefulness in fighting, became a powerful antidote for all poisons. One story tells of animals in the forest who are afraid to drink from a polluted stream. The animals wait until dusk, when a unicorn appears each day. The unicorn dips its horn into the stream and purifies the water, then disappears back into the woods. The animals can then safely drink the water, thanks to the noble unicorn.

Many medieval lords and kings lived in fear of being poisoned by their enemies. In order to purify their food and drink, they went to great expense to buy horns they believed came from unicorns. These "unicorn" horns were fake, of course, but most people still believed. Unicorn horns became known as alicorns. Many alicorns were put on display, or ground into powder and sold as medicine.

Left: A detail from a medieval manuscript showing the capture of a unicorn.
Far right: A fifteenth-century tapestry called *The Unicorn in Captivity.*

Hunting for unicorns in order to obtain their horns was a difficult task. Everyone knew that unicorns fought to the death in order to avoid capture. One trick hunters used was to stand next to a tree, and then provoke a unicorn to charge. At the last moment, the hunter would dodge out of the way. The poor unicorn, who had charged with such fury, would thrust his horn into the tree, becoming hopelessly stuck and at the mercy of the hunter. This was a very dangerous way to hunt unicorns, however, and many a clumsy hunter was killed if he wasn't quick enough to dodge out of the way at just the right moment.

One day, so the legend goes, a unicorn hunter brought his young daughter with him on a unicorn hunt. To his amazement, the unicorn slowly trotted up to his daughter and gently laid his head in her lap. The unicorn became completely tame in the presence of the maiden, and didn't even mind when the hunter sawed off its magical horn. From that day on, maidens were used as bait in order to trick unicorns into giving up their horns. This is why so much artwork of unicorns shows the animals with their heads resting peacefully in a maiden's lap.

Far right: A unicorn statue at Casa Loma, in Toronto, Canada. *Below:* A painting depicting a dangerous unicorn hunt.

UNICORN books AND FILMS

Even today, unicorns continue to fascinate and entertain us. They have appeared in many recent movies and fantasy books. One example is *Nico the Unicorn*, a popular novel by Frank Sacks (made into a movie in 1998) about an 11-year-old boy and his family who adopts a neglected horse from a traveling circus. The horse gives birth to a unicorn, which has magical powers.

Right: The book jacket of *The Last Unicorn*, by Peter S. Beagle.
Below: Harry Potter and the Sorcerer's Stone, by J.K. Rowling.

In *The Last Unicorn*, a novel by Peter S. Beagle, a courageous unicorn and a magician go on a quest to battle an evil king who hates unicorns. The book was turned into a very popular animated film in 1982, and a live-action remake in 2004.

In *Legend*, a 1985 film starring Tom Cruise and featuring a magical world of elves, goblins, and other mythical creatures, the Lord of Darkness tries to bring about eternal night by killing every unicorn in the world.

In *Harry Potter and the Sorcerer's Stone*, Harry is sent into the forbidden forest to find out what is killing the unicorns. He follows a silver trail of blood, then finds a dead unicorn lying on the forest floor. To Harry Potter's horror, a hooded figure crawls across the ground and starts to drink the dead unicorn's silvery, magical blood. The creature then notices Harry and advances on him. At the last moment, Harry is saved by Firenze, a guardian centaur. He tells Harry that the creature that killed the unicorn was drinking the poor beast's blood in order to stay alive. But killing a unicorn is a terrible thing to do, and whoever killed the unicorns of the forbidden forest will lead a cursed life. Harry realizes that the shadowed figure must have been his archenemy, Voldemort, who is trying to stay alive long enough to acquire the Elixir of Life.

Below: A unicorn crosses a river in this illustration by Buddy Mays.

The Search for Real Unicorns

During the sixteenth and seventeenth centuries, people's faith in the reality of unicorns began to fade. Many items that had been sold as alicorns (unicorn horns) were proven to be frauds. Stories about unicorns were beginning to be shown as just that—stories. Still, many people still believed in unicorns, and the search for proof continued.

Many believed that unicorns, which of course were shy and solitary creatures, had fled to lands still unexplored, such as the Americas, or the frigid Arctic wastelands. Indeed, in 1577, Arctic explorer Martin Frobisher discovered a large sea mammal, like a dolphin, with a single horn sprouting from its head. Many people believed that the discovery of this animal, which we know today as the narwhal, proved the existence of unicorns.

In 1663, what appeared to be a unicorn fossil was discovered in a cave near the German town of Quedlinberg. Part of the animal's spine was missing, but the intact skull had a single horn several feet long. The discovery caused quite a sensation. The people of the nearby Harz Mountains told legends of women

Below: The narwhal, a kind of whale, was possibly mistaken long ago for a unicorn.

riding on unicorns, so many thought the discovery proved their existence. Scholars have since come up with many theories about the horn, but most agree that it definitely is not a unicorn. More likely, the scientist who reconstructed the fossil assembled it incorrectly from a collection of ancient mammoth bones.

Despite a lack of hard evidence, many insist that unicorns are real. Why else, they say, would unicorn legends be told for so long? Why is the myth so persistent? Some people say it's not unreasonable to think that unicorns were real creatures once, but died out as human civilization spread. Some even say unicorns still exist in some corner of the world still untouched by humans. After all, they say, new creatures are being discovered every day. For these true believers, unicorns will always be real. For the rest of us, they do exist, but only in our dreams and imagination.

Below: Unicorn Walking Towards Waterfall, by Buddy Mays.

PEGASUS

 egasus was a winged horse from ancient Greek mythology. He is usually shown as a beautiful white steed with huge, golden-colored wings. His name means "strong."

There are two versions of how Pegasus was born. Both state that he is the offspring of the monstrous Gorgon Medusa, the snake-haired woman who could turn men to stone just by the sight of her terrible eyes. When the Greek hero Perseus slew Medusa by cutting off her head, according to one version of the story, Pegasus sprang from the Gorgon's neck, already fully grown. Another version says that Medusa's blood dripped into the sea, where it was turned into Pegasus by Poseidon, the Greek god of the sea.

Below: Starflight by Janny Wurts.

When Pegasus took to the air, he was the swiftest creature on earth, and nobody could catch him, or even come close. Pegasus flew to Mount Helicon, home of the nine Greek muses, where he was welcomed and taken care of. To repay the muses for their kindness, Pegasus used his hooves to dig a spring called Hippocrene. Today, anyone who drinks from the "horse well" is rewarded with artistic inspiration, gifts from the muses and Pegasus.

Another Greek hero, this one named Bellerophon, was given a golden bridle from the goddess Athena. He used the bridle to capture and tame Pegasus. Bellerophon then went on many adventures mounted atop the magical winged horse. One of his first tasks was to destroy the fire-breathing dragon Chimera, which he defeated only after a fierce battle waged in a storm cloud.

After becoming a great hero, Bellerophon attempted to ride to Mount Olympus to take his place among the gods. Zeus, king of the gods, grew angry at Bellerophon's arrogance. He sent down a gadfly to sting Pegasus. The magical horse bucked so hard that Bellerophon fell to earth. The hero became lame and blind from his injuries, but Pegasus continued riderless to Mount Olympus. A constellation of stars was named after him, and he thereafter became the carrier of thunder and lightning for Zeus.

Below: Fireflight by Janny Wurts.

GRIFFINS

riffins are large creatures that are the offspring of lions and eagles. Also called *griffons*, or *gryphons*, they have the bodies of lions, the heads and wings of eagles, and on some accounts, the tail of a serpent. Their hindquarters resemble a lion, but their forelegs end like the talons of an eagle. Griffins are usually much more massive than lions, as much as eight times larger.

Far right: Janny Wurts's *To Ride Hell's Chasm.* *Below: Jeff's Gryphon* by Don Maitz.

Griffins are mentioned in ancient Greek and Asian legends. The myths say that griffins originally lived in the mountains of Asiatic Scythia, which is now part of southern Russia. They also ranged in the desert areas of the Middle East and Mediterranean. Griffins discovered and hoarded gold and jewels, jealously guarding their riches in hidden caves. Anyone who tried to steal the griffins' gold was torn apart by sharp teeth and talons. Ancient Indian legends tell of griffins standing guard against anyone who might plunder a gold mine. Even today, many gold mines are said to still be guarded by griffins, and anyone greedy enough to venture within risks life and limb.

Griffins were also used by the ancient gods, such as Jupiter and Nemesis, to draw their magical chariots. For this reason, the jealous griffons hate horses and prey on them, as well as cows and sheep. A typical griffin can easily carry off a horse in its talons.

Griffins are very popular in heraldry. Their image, a symbol of strength and vigilance, can be found on the coat of arms of many families.

Mermaids

ermaids—along with their mermen mates—are a race of creatures who live in the sea. They are also called sea-maids. Their upper torso, arms and head are human-shaped, but their bottom portion resembles a fish. Most mermaids are extremely beautiful. It's said that they originated along the coast of Brittany, and from there migrated to the British Isles and Scandinavia. They like the cold water of the Atlantic Ocean, and are seldom seen in the tropics. Some have been spotted as far away as North America and China, but they are somewhat different in appearance from their European cousins.

Mermaids live beneath the sea, but they can breath air and can sit for long periods of time on the land. They are intelligent creatures. They have their own language, but they can also speak several human tongues. If the mermaid wishes, it can grow legs and live among humans. Usually, though, mermaids yearn for the sea, and soon return to their watery homes.

Fishermen have often told tales of spotting mermaids. Today many scholars think these sightings were actually of manatees, the gentle cows of the sea, or even of small whales or porpoises.

Far right: A mermaid entices a man in a canoe, in this illustration by Power O'Malley. *Below:* Janny Wurts's *Mariner's Delerium*.

Mermaids have many magical powers. They have a natural ability to find sunken gold, and because of this many human treasure seekers try to make contact with mermaids. Mermaids have also been known to tell fishermen where to catch the biggest fish.

Sometimes mermaids weren't so nice to humans. Another name for mermaid is *siren*. The sirens of ancient mythology used to lie on shore and entice sailors with their music and beauty. Sailors foolish enough to steer their ships close were wrecked on the jagged rocks and sent to their death beneath the deep blue sea.

GLOSSARY

COAT OF ARMS

A piece of artwork that consists of emblems and figures that serve as the special insignia of a person or family, or sometimes an institution. In medieval times, coats of arms often decorated shields, or were printed over a light garment that was worn over armor.

FOLKLORE

The unwritten traditions, legends, and customs of a culture. Folklore is usually passed down by word of mouth from generation to generation.

MARCO POLO

Marco Polo was a merchant and explorer from the present-day city of Venice, Italy. In the late thirteenth century, he was one of the first Europeans to travel to China overland. During his travels he claimed to have encountered creatures that resembled unicorns.

MEDIEVAL

Something from the Middle Ages.

MESOPOTAMIA

Mesopotamia was an ancient country that once was located in southwest Asia. Mesopotamia was situated between the upper Tigris and Euphrates rivers. Today this area is a part of modern Iraq.

MIDDLE AGES

In European history, a period defined by historians as between 476 A.D. and 1450 A.D.

MYTHOLOGY

The study or collection of myths. Myths are traditional stories collected by a culture. Their authors are almost always unknown. Myths explain the origin of mankind, or of civilizations. They also explain the customs or religions of a people. Myths are often stories that include the deeds of gods and great heroes.

PERSIA

Persia was an ancient empire in southwest Asia. It is the former name of the country known today as Iran. The Persian Empire was at its peak around 500 B.C. It occupied an area from the Indus River to the western borders of Asia Minor and Egypt.

RENAISSANCE

A period of European history in the 14th, 15th, and 16th centuries. The Renaissance represented a great revival of learning, art, and literature. It is seen by historians as a bridge between medieval times and the modern world.

Left: An illustration by Janny Wurts from her novel, *To Ride Hell's Chasm.*

Index